Black Woman, Black Woman

Black Woman, Black Woman
Copyright © 2017 by Henry L Singletary. All rights reserved

No part of this publication may be reproduced, stored in a retrieval system or transmitted in any way by any means – electronic, mechanical, photocopy, recording, or otherwise – without the prior permission of the author, except as provided by the USA copyright law.

This book is designed to provide accurate and authoritative information with regard to the subject matter covered. This information is given with the understanding that neither the author, nor Singletary Productions, LLC is engaged in rendering legal, professional advice.

Since the details of your situation are fact dependent, you should additionally seek the services of a competent professional.

Published by Singletary Productions LLC

Edited by Laureen Dunn and Emma Singletary Battle
Raleigh, North Carolina

Book design Copyright © 2017 by Singletary Productions LLC. All rights reserved.

Photography by David Cooper

Published in the United States of America

ISBN: 978-0-692-99914-1

Poetry/Subjects &Themes/Inspirational & Motivational

Black Woman, Black Woman

Dedicated to:

- *My mother Sarah Singletary: Gone but not forgotten you were the first woman I grew to love and learn from. I can never repay you for the sacrifices and care you gave me. You continue to inspire me to be the best that I can be as I go through life. You were not only my mother you were my best friend. I hope this book honors you and dad.*

- *My father Joseph Singletary: You supported me in everything I did in life. You were a great provider and businessman. You taught me so much. I am where I am today because of you.*

- *My grandmother Mary Cooper "Honey": Your love for all of us is still felt today. No one can cook like you. No one will ever be as sweet as you. I miss you so much.*

- *My grandfather Harmon Cooper Sr.: Thank you for taking the time to teach me what life is all about. I miss ridding with you to the store and into town. You told me I could be anything I set my mind to.*

- *My grandmother Corrine Cooper: I can never thank you enough for the love and care you gave me all throughout my life. I miss spending my summers living with you and working with you. You taught me how to love myself by showing me how to respect and love others.*

- *My sister Emma Singletary Battle: You are so talented, very intelligent and smart. You can run any company in the world. I praise the Lord for you. Thank you for the support, you have given me throughout the years.*

- *My sister Sylvia Frasier: When I look at you I see our father. I'm proud of you. Keep spreading the Lord's word. Your book will be coming out soon. God bless you and keep you always.*

- *My sister Angela Singletary Hicks: I can always talk to you when I need a listening ear. When I look at you I see our mother. I'm so proud of you. The Lord has blessed you with a beautiful family. Thank you for helping turn my dreams into a reality. God's peace and blessings to you always.*

Black Woman, Black Woman

- *My sister Jennifer Singletary Stewart: The baby girl. You are so intelligent and sophisticated with your style. You are moving up in the corporate world. God has blessed you with a beautiful family. I'm so proud of you. God's peace and blessings to you always.*

- *My sister Beverly Singletary-Hilliard: You what we all need to aspire to be. You are so sweet, loving and unselfish. Gods peace and blessings to you always.*

- *My aunt Ernestine Cooper: Thank you for your love and support you given me all throughout my years. You always greet me with a smile. May God's peace and blessings be with you always.*

- *My aunt Jannie Eddy Cooper: Thank you for the love and care and direction you gave me throughout the years.*

- *My aunt Ruth McCollough: You have always treated me like one of your kids. I always look forward to coming to visit you and Uncle Knee, May God bless and keep you always.*

- *My cousin Vanessa Pressley: You gave me the confirmation I needed to release this book.*

- *My daughter Alexus Kearney: You will always be the apple of my eye. You are really growing and maturing now. I love you so much. I always enjoy the time we spend together. May God continue to bless and keep you always.*

- *My daughter Shakira Singletary, daddy's baby girl: I love to see you smile when I sing to you. You have become a beautiful young lady. When I look at you I can see myself. I love you so much. May God bless and keep you always.*

- *My uncle David Cooper.:You are my uncle and role model. You have set the standard that we all try to follow. I knew if I just walked in your footsteps I would always be able to stand. Thank you for your love and support you have given me. Thank you for your contribution to this book You have always been there for me. May God bless and keep you always.*

Black Woman, Black Woman

- *My cousin Dr. Trella Cooper, a pediatrician for the towns of Clayton and Smithfield, NC: You are an inspiration to all young women everywhere.*

Bios of those pictured:

- *Angela Singletary Hicks is me sister, a registered nurse, mother of two girls and a beautiful black woman. She enjoys spending time with her family, friends and caring for others.*

- *Antonia Hicks is my niece, a sophomore in college and a beautiful black woman. She enjoys working with people, volunteering in the community and mentoring high school students.*

- *Zaire A. Fritzpatrick is a vibrant and beautiful black woman who aspires to be phenomenal in all of her future endeavors. She enjoys working with children, especially those who are economically challenged. She enjoys creating customized furniture for women and girls, and aspires to be an entrepreneur.*

- *Melvinia ("Mel") is a nurse and clinical administrator of two physician practices. She is a beautiful black woman and mother of two identical twin daughters and a son. She sings in her church choir.*

- *TA-Wanda Mosley IG:Miss30sexxi, Tawndathevixen1@gmail.com is a model available for commercials, music videos and photo shoots.*

Black Woman, Black Woman

About me, the author:

I am a minister, poet, philosopher and motivational speaker who accepted the Lord when I was 9 years old. I got called to preach when I was 16, and have embraced my calling. I read the word of God daily and fast every week. I have a passion for helping people discover God's purpose for their life, and look forward to spreading God's Word through books and speaking. I give thanks and all glory to my Lord and Savior Jesus Christ for the vision and inspiration to write this book.

I am blessed with an entrepreneurial spirit and president of Singletary Productions, which is a provider of inspirational and motivational books, cards, posters and t-shirts. I also own Triangle Maintenance & Janitorial Service, a company that provides commercial and industrial janitorial services throughout the United States. When I am not working or writing, I enjoy playing golf, tennis, fishing and spending time at the beach. I am a graduate of North Carolina Agricultural & Technical State University and a veteran who served four years in the United States Marine Corps.

Contact me for speaking engagements:
SingletaryProductions@gmail.com   (336) 287-1710

Black Woman, Black Woman

Note from the author:

We celebrate the unique beauty of the Black woman all over the world. God created each of you in his own image.

Each one of you are so beautiful, uniquely talented and have your own individual style.

I thank the Lord for all of you. I want to thank all the ladies that appear on the front cover of the book. I want to thank my uncle David Cooper for his outstanding photography work.

I want to thank my dermatologist Dr. Scales for keeping me looking good. His practice is located at the North Carolina Center For Dermatology, in Durham NC. I want to thank the models that appear in the book and the website. I have to acknowledge my alma mater, North Carolina A&T State University. Whenever I am back on campus, I'm always inspired to write something. Some of the content of the book was written while on campus. I will always be indebted to this great university.

May the blessings and peace of Jesus Christ be with all of you always.

Black Woman, Black Woman

BLACK WOMAN, BLACK WOMAN

Singletary Productions, LLC

Black Woman, Black Woman

Contents

Black Woman Black Woman 14-22

Baby Please 23

Baby I Love You 5

My Little Baby Sister 26

Our Love 27

When it comes to you 28

Passion...29

Be Mine 28

Delight...29

Black Woman, Black Woman

The ones with those big sexy hips

The ones with the soft luscious lips

The ones that cause me to stare and make my

Heart stop and skip

Black Woman, Black Woman

The ones that take my breath way

The ones that don't take me serious.

They think I'm just trying to play

Black woman black woman

The ones with those pretty chinky eyes

The ones that don't think they are pretty,

Yet they are any man's prize

Black Woman, Black Woman

The ones with those pretty long legs

I'M TALKING ABOUT ALL YOU FINE SISTAS
THAT MAKE ME BEG

Black Woman, Black Woman

You are what all men want and need

Some of us get selfish and get caught up with greed

Black Woman, Black Woman

Always feel good about what you do

Remember God gave you life and created you.

Black woman black woman

Black Woman, Black Woman

You always make me smile

I'm always blown away by your class and style

Black woman black woman

You are beautiful intelligent God fearing and smart

You are what every man desires in his heart

Black Woman, Black Woman

You are incredible sexy, witty, and smart

You are what every man desires and needs

Always look to God and not feed into greed

Black Woman, Black Woman

The ones with those big sexy thighs

Just loving you makes me high

Black woman black woman

The ones that are so curvy and very filled out

Whenever I look at you I want to shout

Black Woman, Black Woman

The ones that are so pretty and very petite

Being with you is always a treat

Black woman black woman

Black woman black woman

The ones that are so thick and stout

You cause me to praise and shout

Black Woman, Black Woman

Some of y'all are small, brown, dark brown,

caramel, chocolate

Light skin, and tall

It's time we gave God his praise and glory

for creating y'all

Black woman Black woman

Black Woman, Black Woman

Always keep God inside your heart.

He is ready and waiting to give you a new start.

Black woman Black woman

Black Woman, Black Woman

You are my momma, my aunt, my wife, my cousin,
my niece, my sister and my daughter too

God didn't make any other woman as pretty as you

Black woman black woman

Some of you are dark chocolate, light skin and red

You are the woman I'm dreaming about as I lie in bed

Black Woman, Black Woman

They all want be just like you

Always look to God, he'll show you what to do

Black woman black woman

You are the best

Don't you know the Lord created you different from the rest.

Black Woman, Black Woman

Life for you sometimes gets sad

God gave you something special, you so bad.

Black woman black woman

We stand up and applaud you today

You have always been able to handle anything in this

life that comes your way

Black Woman, Black Woman

No other woman is as pretty and sweet

Having you in my life makes me complete

Black woman black woman

It's past time we recognized you

Today I just want to show appreciation for all the

things you do

Black Woman, Black Woman

Be proud of who you are

You are so sexy, talented and intelligent,

you truly are a star

Never compromise your dream you can go far

Black woman black woman

I love to feel your touch

Nothing in this life for you is ever too much

Black Woman, Black Woman

You come in all sizes and shades

You are the best thing in this life that God has

ever made

Black woman black woman

Your beauty is more than skin deep

Nothing in this life for you is ever too steep

Black Woman, Black Woman

Always be who you are

Each one of you are so talented and beautiful,

you truly are a star

Black woman black woman

Let me be your man

United together the two of us can stand

Black Woman, Black Woman

You will always be my choice

Today I'm recognizing you and giving you your voice

Black woman black woman

I never want to let you down

I need you and love you I'm very happy when you

are around

You give me peace whenever I hear your sound

Black Woman, Black Woman

All of you are so pretty and smart

Always look to the Lord when it comes to protecting

your heart

Black Woman, Black Woman

All the other ladies wish they could be just like you

That's why they copy your style, skin tone, features

    and called this something new

They have always been, jealous and envious of you

Black Woman, Black Woman

Dream big and reach for the sky

You will never know how far you will get

if you don't try

Black woman black woman

Remember God will put you on the right track

Keep moving forward and never look back

Black Woman, Black Woman

Always look to the Lord

He'll give you direction and show you the way

With him throughout your life is where you need

to stay

Black woman black woman

You come in all shapes and sizes

Some of you have skin that is

fair and bright

While others of you are caramel and dark and

your color resembles the night

Yet all of you are so pretty I just want to hold you tight

Black Woman, Black Woman

Your beauty is very rare

Loving you is like heaven, please take me there

Black Woman, Black Woman

Baby please understand,

I just want to be your man

I really love it when you are near

If you don't know already, I'm making that very clear

You have no idea how you really make me feel

I'm not playing girl, my love for you is real

I'm hoping and praying, you will always be by my side

Come to me darling, it's time to set aside your pride.

Baby please understand I really want to be your man.

Black Woman, Black Woman

You are the woman I asked the Lord for.

Please don't walk out the door.

I'm sorry I hurt your heart.

What I did wasn't very smart.

Please give us one more chance

Come close to me, let's take advantage of this song and dance

I never want to make you feel this way again

Let's make this our new beginning and let's not make this the end.

My love for you gets stronger each day,

With you is where I always want to stay.

No one can replace you.

Please forgive me, I never meant to make you feel blue.

Baby my love for you is real.

You have no idea how you really make me feel.

Baby you are so pretty, sexy and smart.

You are the woman that has captured my heart.

Right now baby please just take my hand.

Today I want the world to know, you're the woman I love.

I'm your man.

Black Woman, Black Woman

My little baby sister, you are the one that I will always adore.

I always look forward to you coming by and knocking on my door.

I always love to see you smile.

Please stay with me and talk to me for a while

You have grown up now and become very beautiful and smart.

You will always have a special place in my heart.

My little baby sister

I think of you often throughout the day.

I miss the days of our youth when we would talk and play.

You are married now and have a family of your own.

My how fast time has come and gone.

The Lord has blessed you with a very good man.

The two of you together will always stand.

My little baby sister

You always made me smile.

You are so unique, talented and sophisticated with your style.

Today I wanted you to know how proud I am of you.

Always look to the Lord he'll show you what to do.

Black Woman, Black Woman

Someone who's willing to give our love a try.

Someone I'll be true to and never tell a lie.

Someone who I could never love too much.

Someone I always want to kiss and feel their touch.

Someone the Lord made just for me.

Someone I gave my heart to, I am all yours now here is the key.

Someone the Lord choose just for me.

Someone I promise to never make cry

Someone I will always love and protect until

the day I die.

Black Woman, Black Woman

When it comes to you, I know I'll soon grow to care.

From the moment I first laid eyes on you, I couldn't help but stare.

Since I been talking to you, time with you is what I want to share.

I think the two of us will make a very perfect pair.

There is no need to, I'll always treat you more than just fair.

You can depend on me because I'll always be there.

Because truly when it comes to you, I know without a doubt I will soon grow to care.

Black Woman, Black Woman

You are quite a lady of fashion

One with plenty of passion.

I can tell by your actions,

You will fill me with complete satisfaction.

Black Woman, Black Woman

Baby I can't get you off of my mind, not only are you
beautiful, baby you just fine
Please don't go away.
With me is where I want you to always stay.
I know you have been hurt before
Please don't leave,
stay with me, please don't walk out the door.
You are the woman, I have been praying and asking
the Lord for.
I promise to love you more and more each day.
That's why with me is where you need to stay.
Baby I really want you to be mine.
I just can't get you off of my mind.
I do really want to hold you tight.
I want to have you forever, not just for this night.
You look so good to me,
When I kissed your lips, I was set free.
Baby please be mine
Girl you are so pretty and sexy, Baby you just fine.
Baby I really do know how you feel, my love for you
is real.
Baby please don't go away, I'm begging you
please stay.

Black Woman, Black Woman

You're quite a delightful sight on this or any night.
I must admit when you first came into my sight, I instantly wanted to hold you so tight,
You know why, I knew you would fit just right.
And every time I look into your beautiful eyes I must admit, I can't help but see a lovely sight.
I do want to hold you, but more than just for one night.
Perhaps the two of us will allow our love to take flight.
There's no need to worry, whatever you and I may do will always work out just right.
And from this moment forward, whenever I think about you. You will always remind me of a delight.

Black Woman, Black Woman

Copyright© 2017 by Henry L Singletary. All rights reserved

No part of this publication may be reproduced, stored in a retrieval system or transmitted in any way by any means - electronic, mechanical, photocopy, recording, or otherwise - without the prior permission of the author, except as provided by the USA copyright law.

The opinions expressed by the author are not necessarily those of Singletary Productions, LLC.

www.ingramcontent.com/pod-product-compliance
Lightning Source LLC
LaVergne TN
LVHW051513070426
835507LV00022B/3087